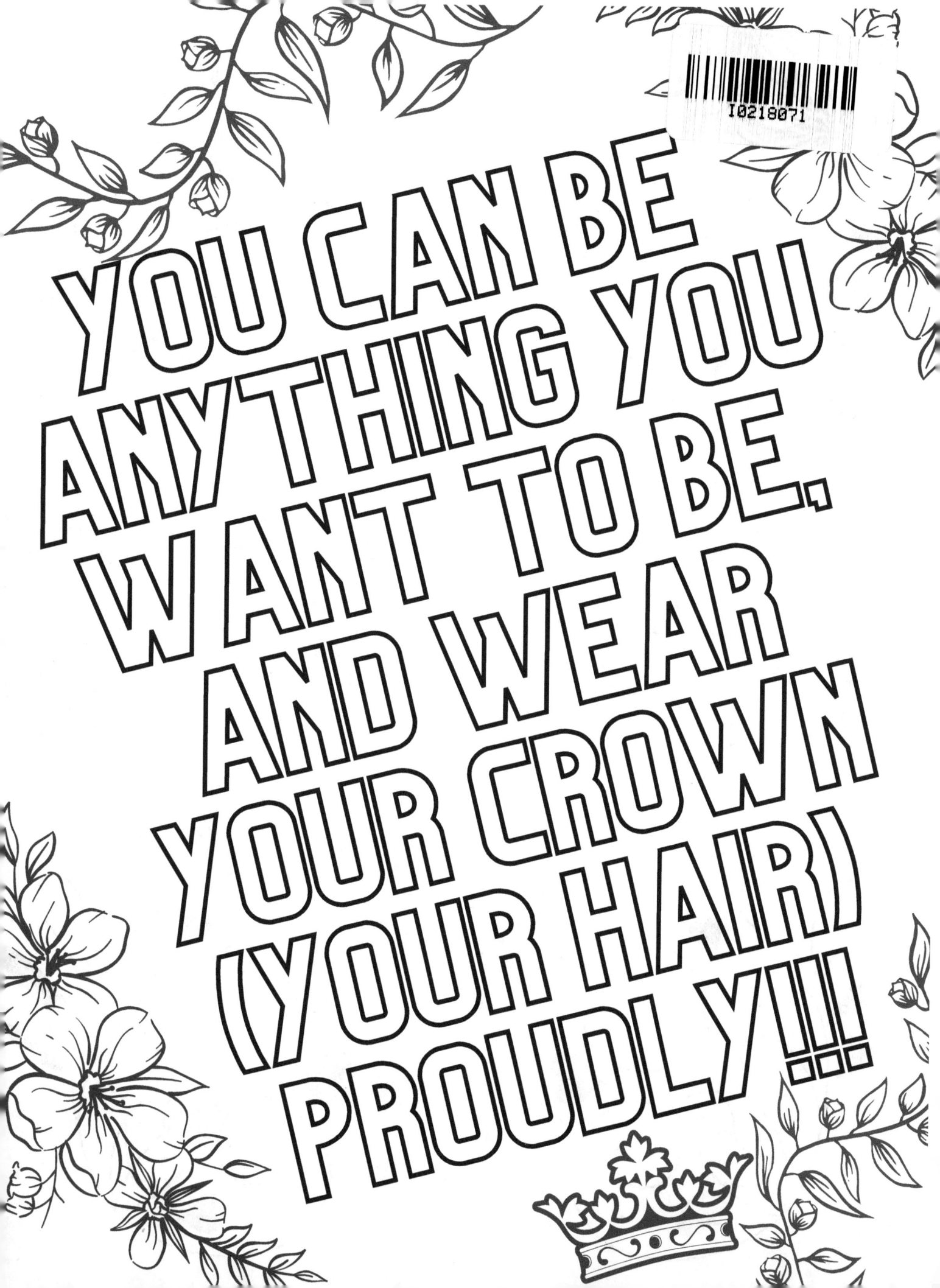

LIL GIRLFRIENDS PICK A CAREER

Lil Girlfriends Pick A Career
Coloring Book
Created & Published 2021
by 2wo Scoops ENT, LLC
All rights reserved.
ISBN: 978-1-7373158-6-5

Send your Lil Girlfriends coloring pages you want featured on 2woscoopspublished.com to

lilgirlfriendsbooks@gmail.com

Shay chose to be an x-ray tech.

Nola chose to be a lawyer.

Draw your favorite hairstyle. Finish the face. Color.

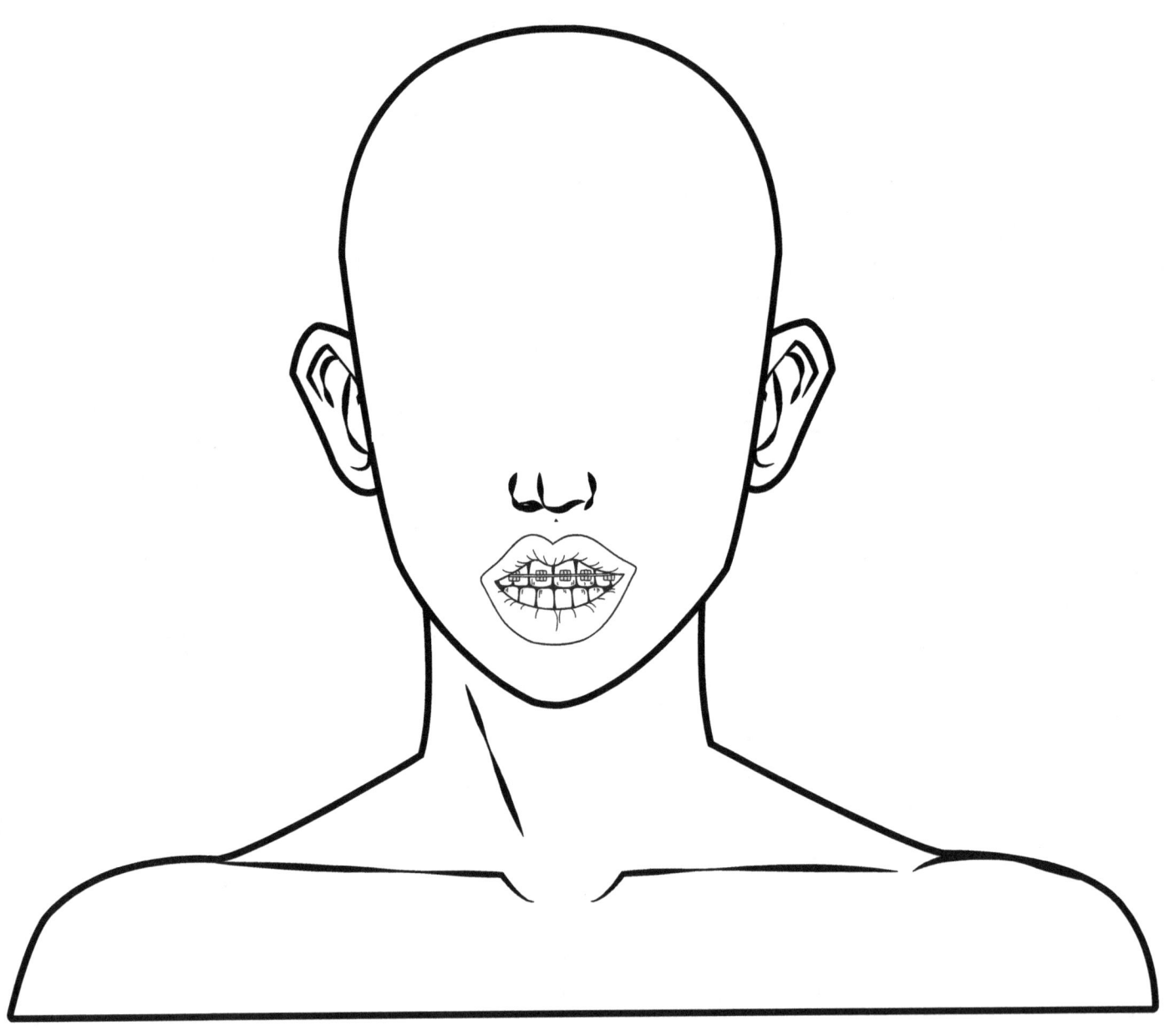

Be Creative

Send your Lil Girlfriends coloring pages you want featured on 2woscoopspublished.com to
lilgirlfriendsbooks@gmail.com

Mikayla chose to be a firefighter.

Career Princess Crossword Puzzle

Down:
2. a lady in the military
3. a Princess's Mother
4. _____ Girl Magic!
8. a lady that paints art
9. a lady that flies in outer space

Across:
1. a Queen & King's daughter
5. your BFF - Best _____ Forever
6. a lady that fixes cars
7. a dancer that wears a tutu
10. a female sibling
11. the lady you visit when you're sick
12. subject in school that uses numbers

#1 Across:

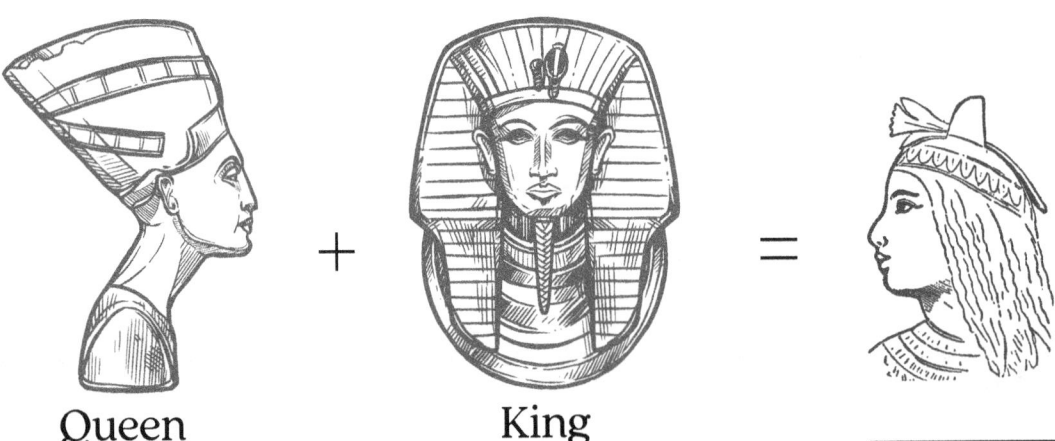

Queen + King = _____

Tiffany chose to be a track champion.

Alexis chose to be a teacher.

Deanna chose to be a police officer.

Send your Lil Girlfriends coloring pages you want featured on 2woscoopspublished.com to
lilgirlfriendsbooks@gmail.com

Match the Princess with the tools she may need for her career. Color.

Laila chose to be a superhero.

Kimber chose to be an eye doctor.

Draw your favorite hairstyle, add a hat or a crown. Finish the face. Color.

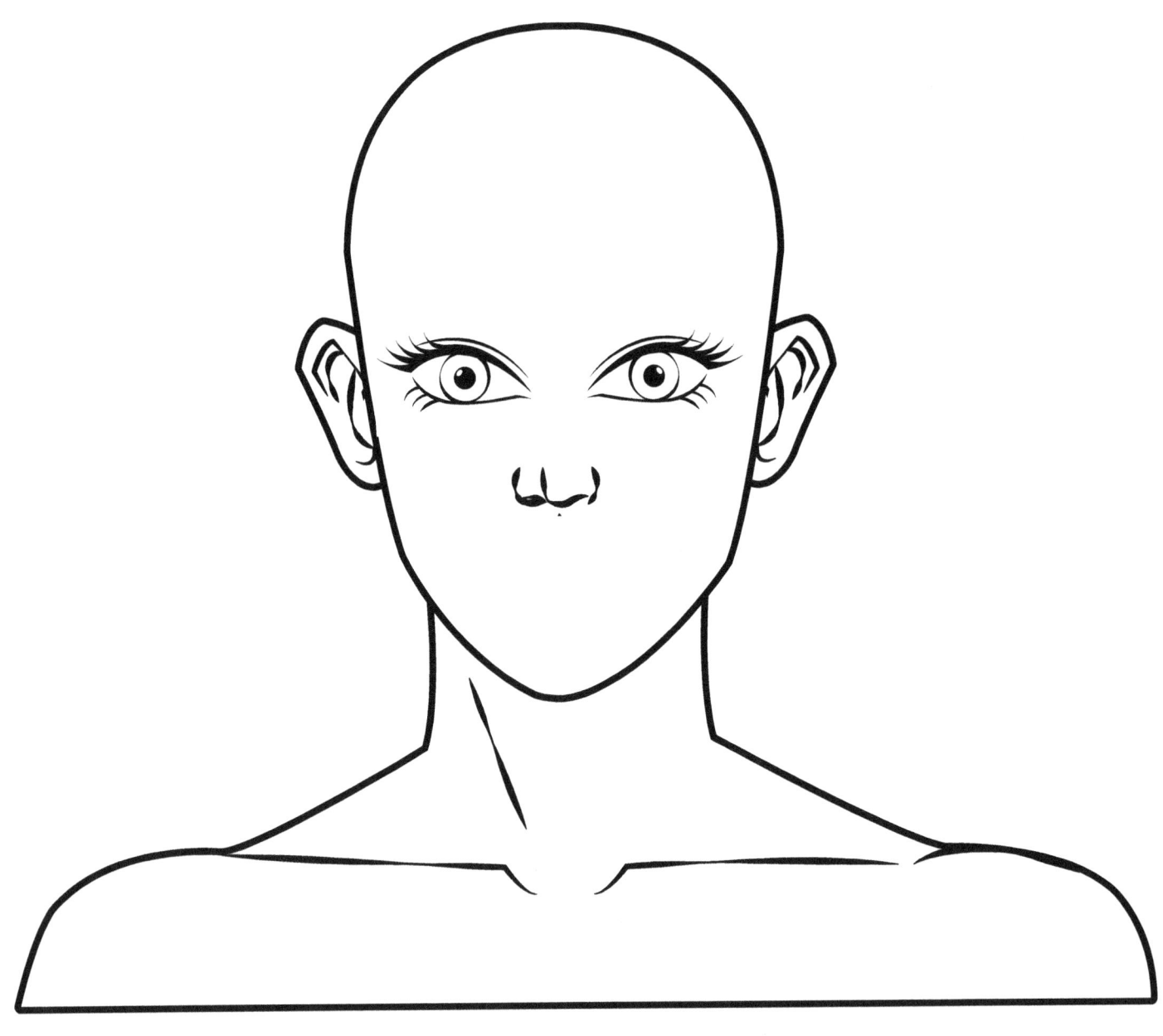

Be Creative

Send your Lil Girlfriends coloring pages you want featured on 2woscoopspublished.com to
lilgirlfriendsbooks@gmail.com

Zara chose to be an artist.

Brittany chose to be a baker.

Amber chose to be a chemist.

Beautiful Black Hair Word Search

```
K D Y N A T U R A L K U T X B
N E F N W P K B R A I D S B J
O J A F R O Q O E K W K D E X
T M L H W R H B L U T S A A D
S P O N Y T A I L Q I O Z D C
P D C P A D P S E E I Q E S R
P N S M Z F Z I C U R L Y R O
S P N V X D R P G E R N O Z W
K T L Q Y O Y O W T L K S P N
K B T W I S T S P X A W H Y Y
M B D H Y L X B K U I I X W M
Z U C X O C L V B G F V L C N
X N E T B L O W O U T F C S O
K I N K Y C J N W R R Q S E F
S X X Y M A E Q S Y N K N V L
```

AFRO PUFFS	PONYTAIL	PIGTAILS	BLOW OUT
NATURAL	TWISTS	BRAIDS	CROWN
KINKY	CURLY	AFRO	KNOTS
BEADS	LOCS	BOWS	BUN

Give her a beautiful hairstyle and do her makeup. Color.

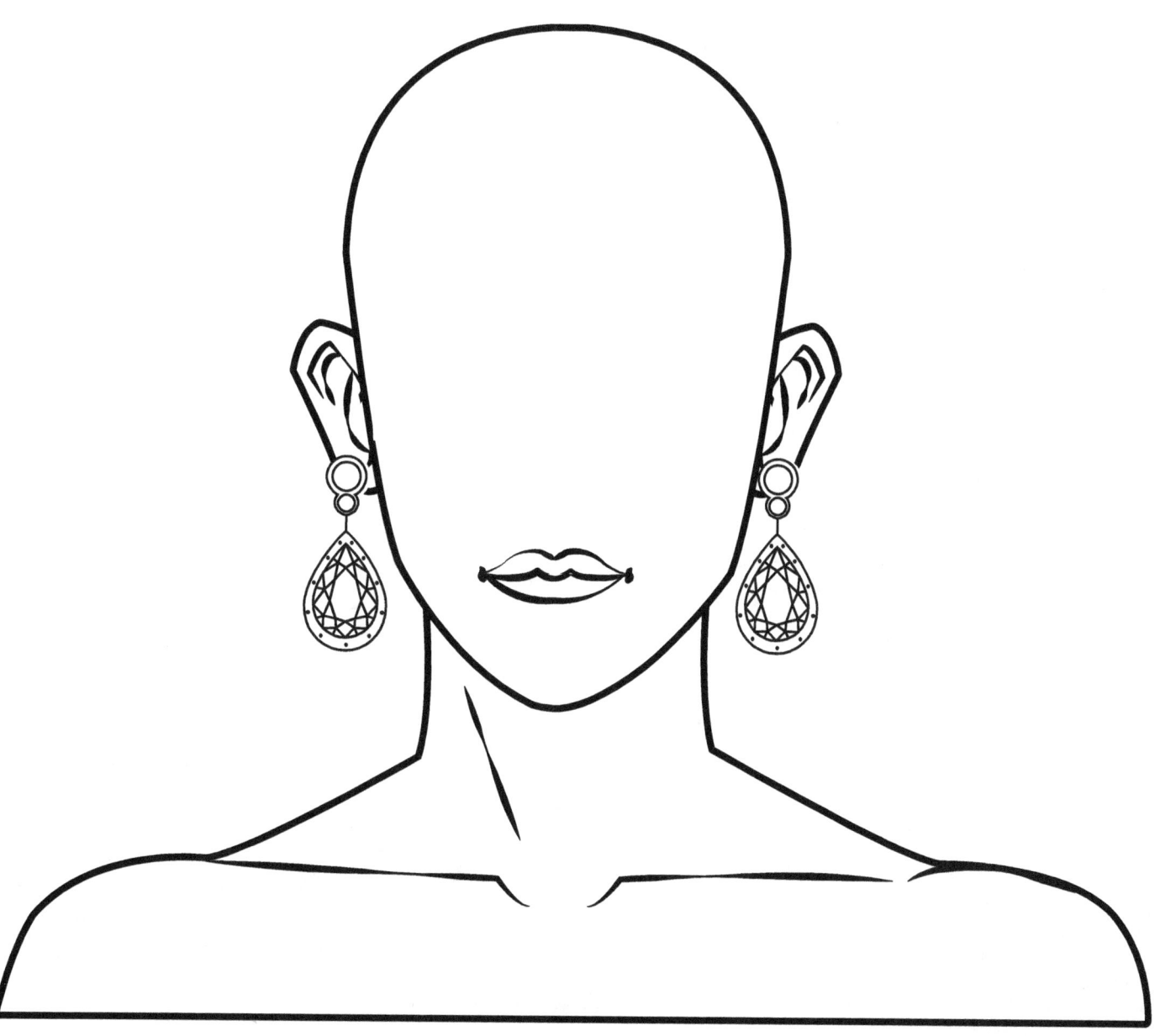

Be Creative

Send your Lil Girlfriends coloring pages you want featured on 2woscoopspublished.com to
lilgirlfriendsbooks@gmail.com

Jayda chose to be a dogwalker.

Kiara chose to be an astronaut.

What is your favorite hairstyle from a movie? Draw it here. Finish the face. Color.

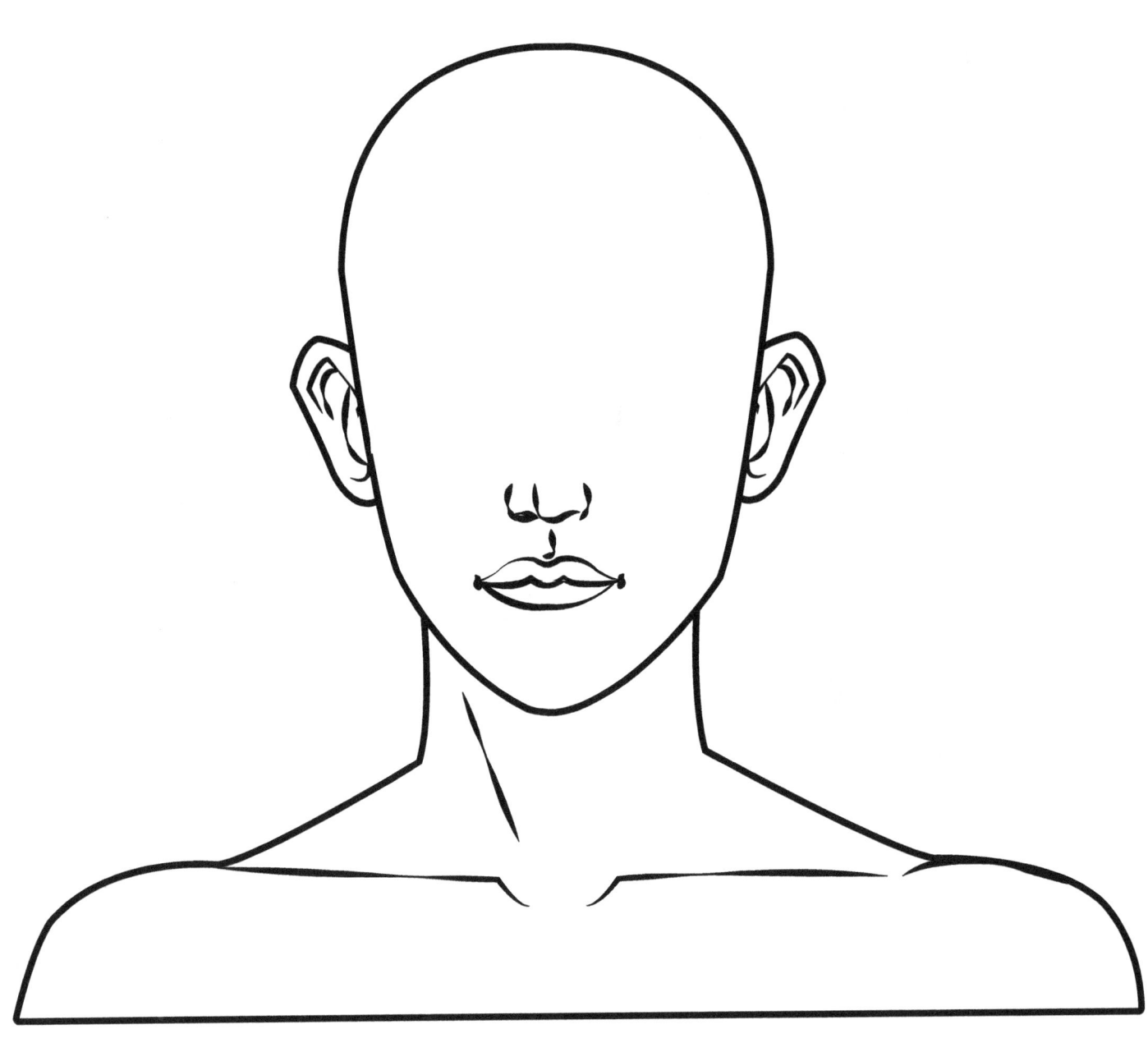

Be Creative

Felicia chose to be a farmer.

Count & color.

6

7

8

9

10

Chelsea chose to be mechanic.

Olivia chose to be a ballerina.

Free face, do what you want. Be creative! Color.

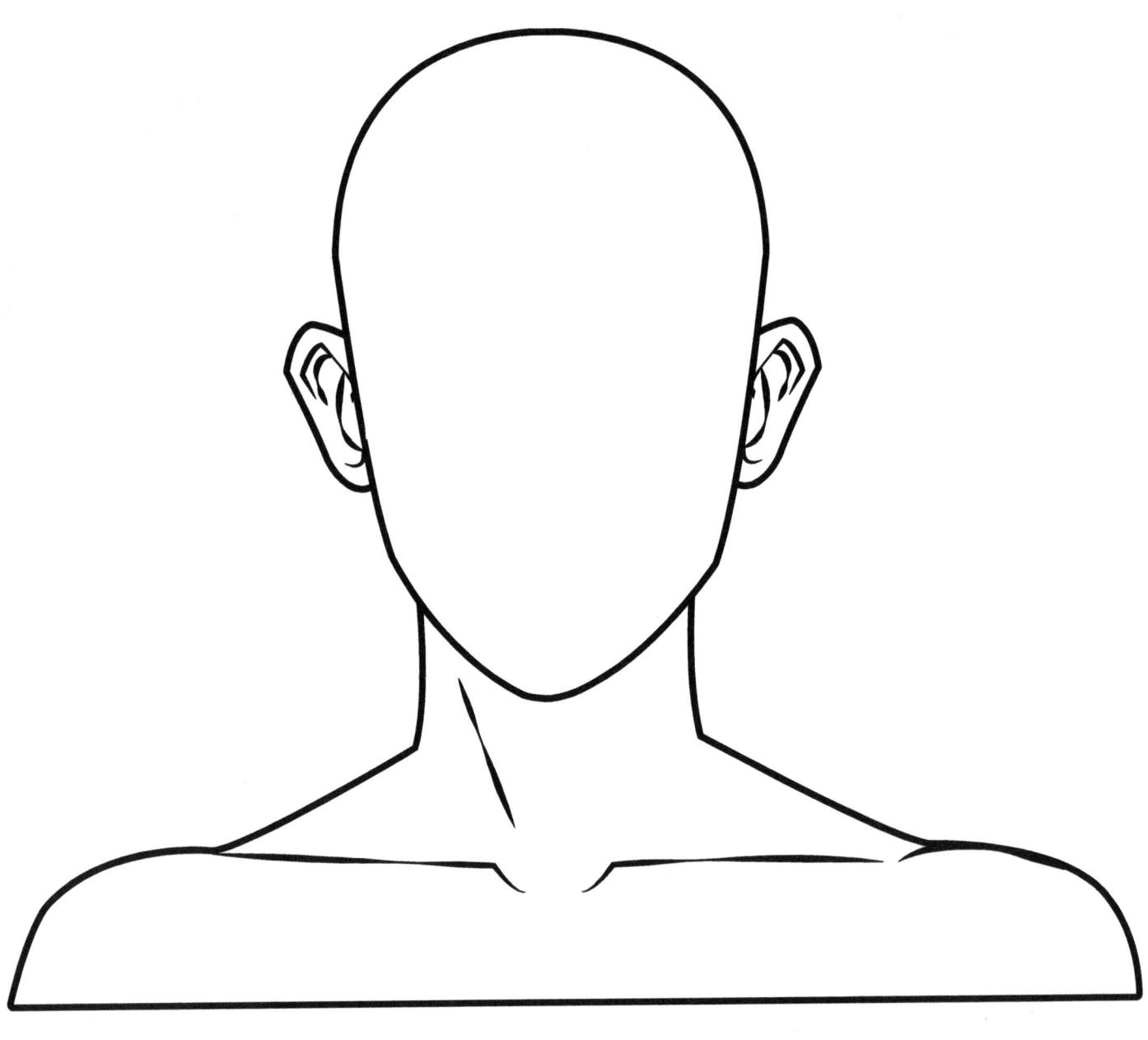

Be Creative

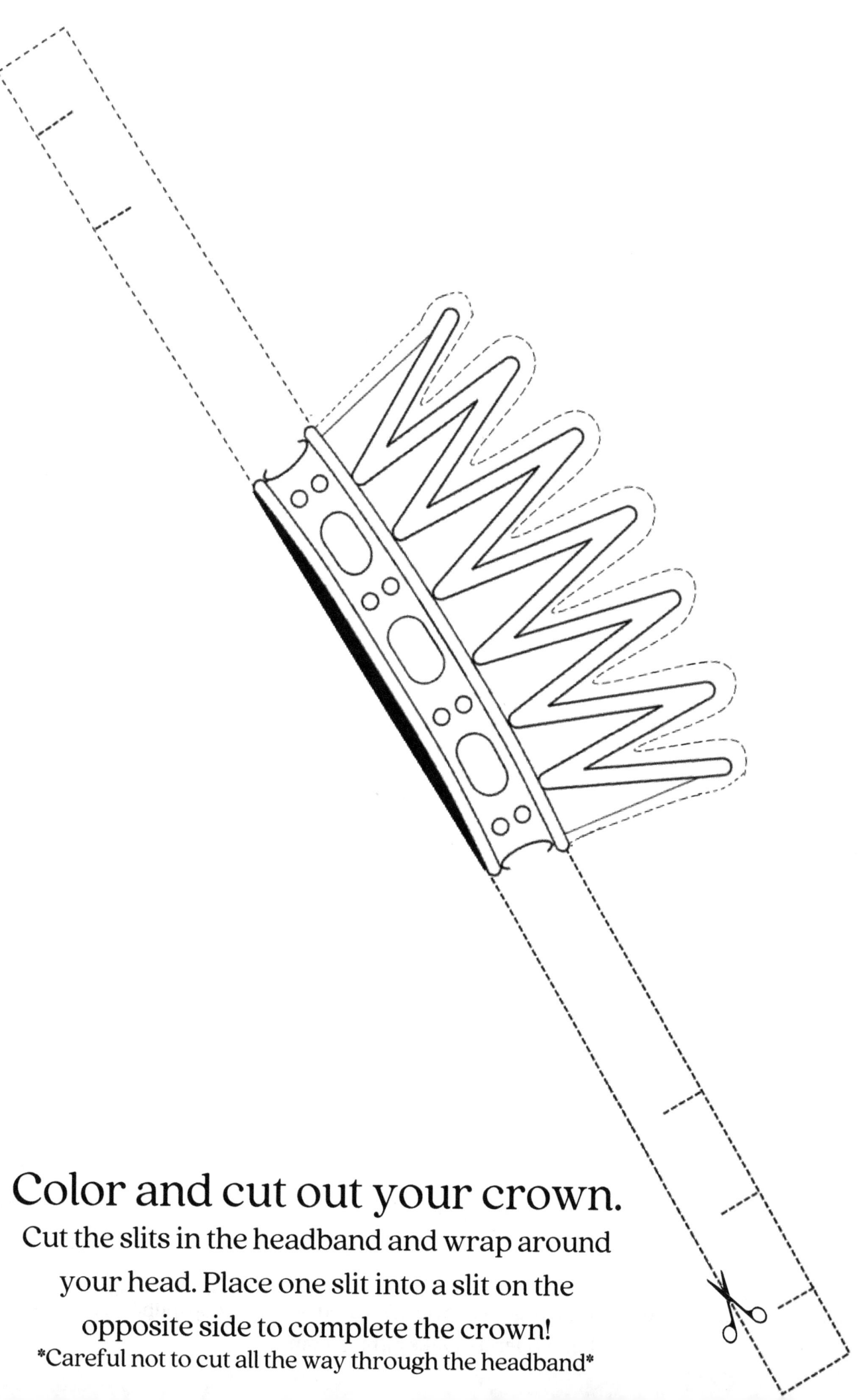

Color and cut out your crown.

Cut the slits in the headband and wrap around
your head. Place one slit into a slit on the
opposite side to complete the crown!
Careful not to cut all the way through the headband

Send your Lil Girlfriends coloring pages you want featured on 2woscoopspublished.com to **lilgirlfriendsbooks@gmail.com**

Send your Lil Girlfriends coloring pages you want featured on 2woscoopspublished.com to **lilgirlfriendsbooks@gmail.com**

BELIEVE IN YOURSELF

KEEP GOING

DON'T QUIT

ON

KNOW YOUR WORTH

THINK IT, WANT IT, GET IT

DO WHAT YOU LOVE

BE BRAVE

YOU CAN SLOW AND STEADY

STAY STRONG & POWER ON

DO YOUR THING